IS IT RIGGED?

V. Agnelli Jr.

ISBN: 1539148246
ISBN-13: 978-1539148241

DEDICATION

Dedicated to those who have the intestinal fortitude of Diogenes and his lamp. May you never give up looking.

CONTENTS

Acknowledgments   i

1 The Challenge   1

2 Northern Virginia (Region One)   8
    8th, 10th, and 11th Districts

3 Elements of The Rural Western Section   34

4 The Southeastern Corner   40

5 Summing up the Possible Fraud   44

6 Suggestions   48

ACKNOWLEDGMENTS

Thanks to those of who have provided support and encouragement to handle this project and to those whom are working in the spirit of the Associations of Freeholders and Freemen to wrest control of our runaway government here in Virginia. May your success be our future as it was given to us in the Virginia Declaration of Rights, Section VI:

" That elections of members to serve as representatives of the people in assembly ought to be free; and that all men, having sufficient evidence of permanent common interest with, and attachment to, the community have the right of suffrage and cannot be taxed or deprived of their property for public uses without their own consent or that of their representatives so elected, nor bound by any law to which they have not, in like manner, assented, for the public good."

June 12, 1776

1 THE CHALLENGE

Being able to vote and voting in every election since the 1980 General Election, I became suspicious of who counts the votes and how they are counted. Since 1980, our nation has watched the most contested general elections in our nation's history. Regular Americans on an ever-increasing basis, thanks to modern technologies, are bringing forward this evidence of election fraud and voter fraud.

Since the 2000 General Election, it appears that one political party has gone to extreme lengths to disrupt that idea first given to us in 1776. We can clearly find out about elections and how they are outlined as to who should participate in them through section VI of the declaration:

"that all men, having sufficient evidence of permanent common interest with, and attachment to, the community have the right of suffrage and cannot be taxed or deprived of their property for public uses without their own consent or that of their representatives so elected"

It is in the spirit of the Declaration of Rights that I exercise my right to audit and be critical of Virginia's election process and its results. I do so out of my "common interest with, and attachment to, the community".

During the 2012 General Election, we watched the results coming in after the polls closed in Virginia. One "event", which has been occurring many times after the 2000 General Election, was that the 8th District votes were always delayed in coming out. Election after election since 2006 appeared to teeter on the vote totals coming from the 8th Congressional District. By the 2012 elections, I had decided to watch the returns carefully through the Virginia Board of Elections' website. After watching the close race slip away to the 8th District, something did not look right again. The following days I made a point of checking back to the website to look at the Absentee and Provisional votes, which might send the race one way or another. As it turns out, it only increased the margins of the victors and in some cases, greatly.

Many people were concerned with the newly allowed form of voting called "provisional" voting. This law goes around the pre-existing law that established a deadline to register for voting. Responsible people follow laws and do not skirt them because they need more convenience than the rest of us. Likewise, we are responsible and are due the protection of the right of suffrage by section VI in the Declaration of Rights. It is in our "common interest with, and attachment to the community" to protect integrity of this right. Our willingness to follow the law is evidence of our wish that our rights are permanent. As it turns out, in 2012, the Provisional voting was a small fraction of vote percentage; however, it still negates our permanent rights by that percentage. The practice of Provisional Voting is nothing more than an open invitation to massive "Voter Fraud" in the future.

"Voter Fraud," as it is referred to, can be institutionalized. Busloads of people can be driven from polling precinct to polling precinct with people who have falsified identifications and or multiple voter registrations. This practice may or may not be as easy as one thinks. It could only happen in jurisdictions where there are friends to the fraudsters. This also defines them as accomplices. It can have devastating effects on election results. I am certain "voter fraud" takes place in Virginia; however, I do not believe it is the largest form in our state.

"Election Fraud," as it is referred to, is an institution. In fact, it would be as serious a crime as treason. It negates all of our votes. It destroys the integrity of an entire election. It is best described as a conspiracy from the inside of government itself. If it were a business, it would be called "pilferage". We know that stealing our vote from our voting booth is infinitely more serious than pilfering stock from the shelves of a store or materials your business uses from day-to-day. It is more serious than stealing money from any business or person. Election Fraud can be responsible for the destruction of a state and the nation to which it belongs. It can result in a nation being fooled into thinking its moral compass has changed from over 2,000 years of practice in just 8 years. Millions of innocent babies could be murdered in what was (until just over one hundred years ago) considered the safest place for a child since the beginning of mankind. The womb is no longer safe thanks to Election Fraud. The right of the people to govern themselves through referendum has been nullified. Federalism itself has been turned around and used as a weapon against us all and because "we the people" choose to be numb to the possibility that anything such as Election Fraud could be possible in our state.

It is my opinion that a combination of Election Fraud and Voter Fraud have taken over Virginia's election process. I will attempt to lay out the facts for you as I have found them from my research. I will then make a list of what I consider to be anomalies. Then I will give my opinion on how these came about. Lastly, I will give my opinion for solutions to stop the Fraud.

All of my raw data was taken from the Virginia Board of Elections website: http://elections.virginia.gov/ you must be aware, however that the Virginia Government has redesigned that website and all of the data I was able to take from it, is not available as of this date, 9/22/16. I printed my documents to work with them by hand and thereby have a scan of the most important data table, entitled "November 6, 2012 General Election Official Results". The table was found under the tab entitled "Voter Turnout Report". It is this report I was unable to find today as I attempted to access it again. I last accessed that page on 8/29/2016.

The area, which first drew my attention that fraud was committed in the 2012 Virginia Election, was the data showing that the 8th District Absentee voting percentage was nearly twice that of the average from the rest of the Commonwealth. It drew me to focus this investigation on the Absentee voting results as a "tell" that Fraud had taken place. If you have played poker or chess, then you know what a "tell" is.

Once I began to break down the very complex district and precinct level voting results, I saw another type pattern emerge in the results. I decided it was necessary to investigate other areas around the state to find out if what I had suspected might not just be localized Fraud to

Northern Virginia.

Unfortunately, based on my analysis, we have a statewide problem. What one might think is a "safe bet" for Republicans in Rural Districts and should not warrant those citizens to suspect problems in their local election boards turns out to be a false sense of integrity.

I will break down the data from Northern Virginia out of elements of the 8th, 10th and 11th Districts. Because they are so intertwined in the same jurisdictions they hold easy comparisons of voter behavior patterns. I will also break them down jurisdiction by jurisdiction. After I break down the situation in Northern Virginia, I will then show the results from two other areas around the Commonwealth for study. I chose these two other areas (regions) for their unlikely commonality to Northern Virginia with the exception they are all part of Virginia.

The first region, has three counties, who share the same physical sections of foothills and mountain region of Virginia, though they are not bordered by each other and provide a pool of data large enough to use for comparison purposes. They have similar size populations. They are mostly rural and have a large portion of their land mass involved in agriculture and tourism.

The second region, is made up of two incorporated cities, shares a common boundary, and has arguably the largest military population in the Commonwealth. It has some of the largest series of Naval Bases in the nation and provides what should be the largest expected percentage of absentee votes in the Commonwealth, per the military personnel deployments. They also have the largest tourist destination in the Commonwealth. It is a perfect hybrid of the rural area's tourism and Northern Virginia's heavy reliance on Federal Government employment.

From the raw data, I will provide quick references on each individual jurisdiction for the total votes on the Presidential, Senatorial, and Congressional races. I will then show the percentages for the top two candidates in the total vote status. Then I will provide the total absentee votes and those percentages.

Here is the area where I found suspicious votes. The percentages in every case may not appear to be too serious. However, consider it happens in almost every case and that should concern you greatly. If you do not see your City or County listed here, then you should go to the Election Results website, review your jurisdiction's performance, and compare them to my findings here.

To bring out the suspicious activity, you should look for a difference of more than 2% in the results between the "On-site" vote totals for the candidate and the "Absentee" vote totals for the same. The Election website provides these percentages for Absentee votes further down in the results. You must follow the link from your Jurisdiction to the precinct level. You will find the Absentee votes are counted in the next to last precinct. There, you can find the votes per candidate and the percentages of votes. Unfortunately, thanks to the out-of-date Voting Rights Act, you may find yourself tabulating each district by hand in counties where more than one Congressional District is shared. I found this challenging at best and our Commonwealth is not allowing jurisdictions to get representation by way of regional interest. Those who were supposedly being protected are being isolated. That is another battle for another day.

Let us start with the general over view of the challenge by looking at the previously mentioned table, "Voter Turnout Report." (Table 1)

• VIRGINIA •
STATE BOARD
of ELECTIONS

SBE Home

November 6, 2012 General Election Official Results

| President | Congress | Referendums | Local Office | Voter Turnout Report | My County / City |

Congressional District | Congressional Locality

District	Active Registered	Total Registered	In Person	In Person Curbside	Absentee	Provisional	Total Voted	% Active Voter Turnout	% Total Voter Turnout
01	451,339	500,180	323,493	1,207	43,700	959	369,359	81.84%	73.85%
02	419,299	484,243	286,211	3,931	30,194	1,138	321,474	76.67%	66.39%
03	408,706	475,353	301,846	3,369	30,136	1,405	336,756	82.40%	70.84%
04	448,665	495,503	324,620	1,439	38,612	1,270	365,941	81.56%	73.85%
05	454,901	502,492	329,837	1,408	35,051	475	366,771	80.63%	72.99%
06	428,015	478,708	311,840	795	27,092	617	340,344	79.52%	71.10%
07	472,921	512,391	356,803	930	37,870	911	396,514	83.84%	77.39%
08	439,694	517,327	287,440	365	74,181	1,554	363,540	82.68%	70.27%
09	433,452	476,478	292,662	703	24,264	276	317,905	73.34%	66.72%
10	457,094	503,131	318,939	407	55,981	889	376,216	82.31%	74.77%
11	434,511	483,027	290,026	517	50,826	657	342,026	78.72%	70.81%
District Totals	4,848,597	5,428,833	3,423,717	15,071	447,907	10,151	3,896,846	80.37%	71.78%

Now I will break that "Absentee" column down for you from the highest percentage to the lowest percentage by district in the data field below: (Table 2)

Absentee Votes per District
By Percentage of Total District Votes

8th District Absentee Votes 23.16

10th District Absentee Votes 14.88

11th District Absentee Votes 14.86

1st District Absentee Votes 11.83

4th District Absentee Votes 10.55

7th District Absentee Votes   9.55

5th District Absentee Votes   9.55

2nd District Absentee Votes   9.39

3rd District Absentee Votes   8.95

6th District Absentee Votes   7.96

9th District Absentee Votes   7.63

As you can see, the unbelievably huge number of Absentee votes is in Northern Virginia. When looking at a map of the 8th Congressional District of Virginia, you see it is probably the smallest of all Virginia's districts because of its high density of population. It is the closest to the Federal Government and the jobs which are associated with it. It has the shortest commuting distances to those jobs and has the shortest distances to its polling precincts. Its citizens should have the least excuse for not being able to make it to the polls on polling day and should have the lowest absentee count in the Commonwealth and not almost two times the Commonwealth's mean average.

As I previously mentioned, the surrounding jurisdictions geographically are broken up to share with adjoining districts. This makes for tangled results, which can make breaking data down, a difficult chore. I will break those down in the next chapter.

For the final quick reference of the data, which is the best visual aid I could think of to show you why there must have been

Election Fraud in Virginia's 2012 General Election; I have enclosed it below and it is titled "2012 Virginia Absentee Ballot": (Graph 1)

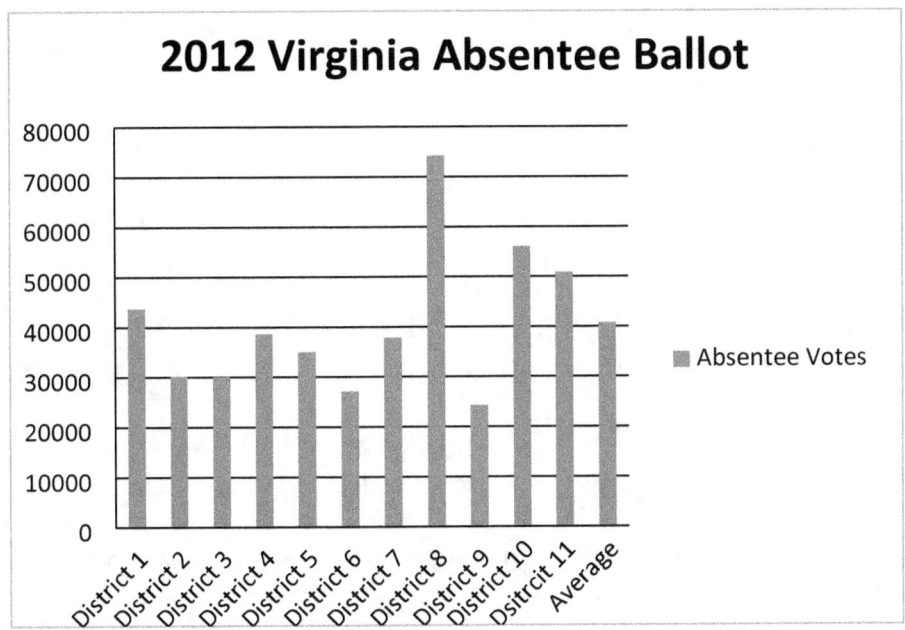

I will utilize this style of chart throughout the book though it may at times not reflect the slight "spreads" of votes between On-site and Absentee voting percentages; however, it will help more in those cases in which the spreads are unusually large.

2 NORTHERN VIRGINIA (REGION ONE) 8TH, 10TH AND 11TH CONGRESSIONAL DISTRICTS

Northern Virginia (as those who call the Commonwealth their domicile know it) is the "big kahuna" of politics and money in Virginia. The people of other parts of the state think the state could not exist without them and Northern Virginia is filled with hot air and people of great self-importance. The people of Northern Virginia think they walk on water or close to it and when it comes to the direction of the state politically, they do.

I have a few theories as to how Election Fraud is being carried out in Virginia and I am not going to blame any particular party. If you follow the numbers from this chapter into the subsequent chapters, you will see why.

To lay out the substrate for the composition of my theories, I want to give my own thoughts and observations on the regions and their physical make up per my 56 years of living in Virginia, visiting and exploring the state as I have. You may or may not agree with my views or you may think them incomplete or overdone. For that, I beg your pardon in advance.

The 8th Congressional District is made up of the City of Alexandria, Arlington County, the City of Falls Church and an eastern portion of neighboring Fairfax County. This portion of Virginia has had the oldest, contiguous population in the Commonwealth, which has never changed from its bearing of importance but only increased it. This area is not like Yorktown or Williamsburg, which rose up and then deflated somewhat into the shadow of Richmond from 1776 and beyond. Therefore, I can say with great confidence, that the 8th district has the largest population of dead people in Virginia. It is probably second only to the 2nd Congressional District population in transient residents related to the military. The exception is their port of call is always in their area at the headquarters of all of the armed services, so they would not have any reason for such a large number of absentee ballots as you would expect from the 2nd District. The 8th District is probably the most compact Virginia Congressional District geographically. It is a high density area and was driven to be that way by eager developers who began their quest in the 1960's and have never given up.

I feel very confident when I claim the 8th District has the highest international population whose ancestors had little or nothing to do with the settling of Virginia or its growth until the last quarter of the 20th Century. The population has the oldest white race population in Virginia. The public school systems show exactly what race is largest and we know it is no longer those of the white race.

To work with the data from this district and try to find out if the incredible claim by the Virginia Board Elections that the 8th District's 74,181 Absentee votes were legitimate, I had to break down the jurisdictional counts from the precinct level.

The one great challenge was Fairfax County. Their population always teeters near or probably over one million people (including those who do not like to be counted in the census). They are split into three different congressional districts. They are the 8th, 10th and 11th. You will see me refer to the same Fairfax County graph in the breakdown of each of those districts so do not be alarmed if you see it repeated. It may actually help not to shield you from the results because it will show a strange phenomenon that would not have been visible if the data was isolated.

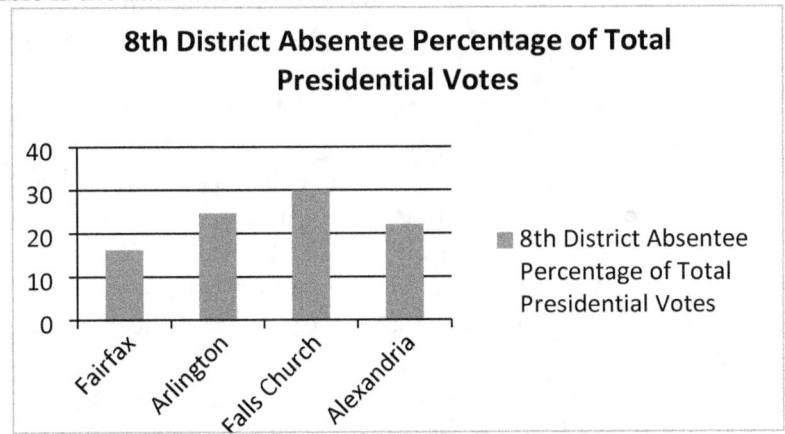

(Chart 2-previous page) shows the breakdown of absentee votes between the four jurisdictions for the office of President, which make up the 8th Congressional District of Virginia. The percentage shows who is most suspect of leading the fraud in the district. By the number of actual votes, Fairfax and Arlington provided far more absentee votes than the City of Falls Church.

(Table 3 below) Covers the breakdown of Total votes and absentee votes. Here are two immediate problems I found with the published results from the Election Board.

District 8 Breakdown of Absentee Vote ratio for Fairfax County, Falls Church City, Alexandria City and Arlington County using the Presidential votes against the published district level totals:

Fairfax Total Votes: 162,112   Absentee Votes: 26,232   Absentee % 16.18
Falls Church Total Votes: 7,276 Absentee Votes: 2,176   Absentee % 29.90
Alexandria Total Votes: 73,411   Absentee Votes: 16,131   Absentee % 21.97
Arlington Total Votes: 117,608   Absentee Votes: 28,954   Absentee % 24.62

Total Votes: 360,407   Total Votes: 73,493   Total % 23.16

I had to print out the precinct level information and tabulate the votes manually to separate the districts in Fairfax County, since they were separated by their districts numerically and not geographically. The precincts were catalogued by their assigned precinct numbers, which are not separated by the various districts across the county. I see no logic to their act of not separating the precincts in geographical groups. The new website, which was activated two days before I wrote this, may or may not correct that problem. I have yet to visit those links to make a comparison.

The first anomaly, comes from comparing the precinct level tabulated votes to the published general page of data from the midlevel-linked pages showing general results from each jurisdiction. That is to say one can reasonably expect that the total votes in a Presidential election would favor the votes for the race of the Presidency over all other contests on the same ballot. One would expect the high number of votes in that race to be the published "Total Votes" from any jurisdiction.

If you revisit (Table 1) "Voter Turnout Report" on page 5, you would do well to look for two figures for the 8th District. The first is

"Total Voted," which is 363,540 and second is "Absentee," which is 74,181.

Doing your basic comparison, you find that the "Voter Turnout Report" published amount is 3,133 more votes than can be summed up from the Precinct level published results for the Presidential race found in the individual jurisdictions.

The second anomaly comes when you compare the "Voter Turnout Report" published for Absentee Ballots of the 8th District and the Precinct level published results from the individual jurisdictions. "The Voter Turnout" page published 688 more votes than you can tabulate from the precinct level tabulations.

This leaves the precinct level tabulations showing a Presidential Vote Total of 360,407 and the Absentee total of 73,493. I will bring up my questions to this in the conclusion section of this book.

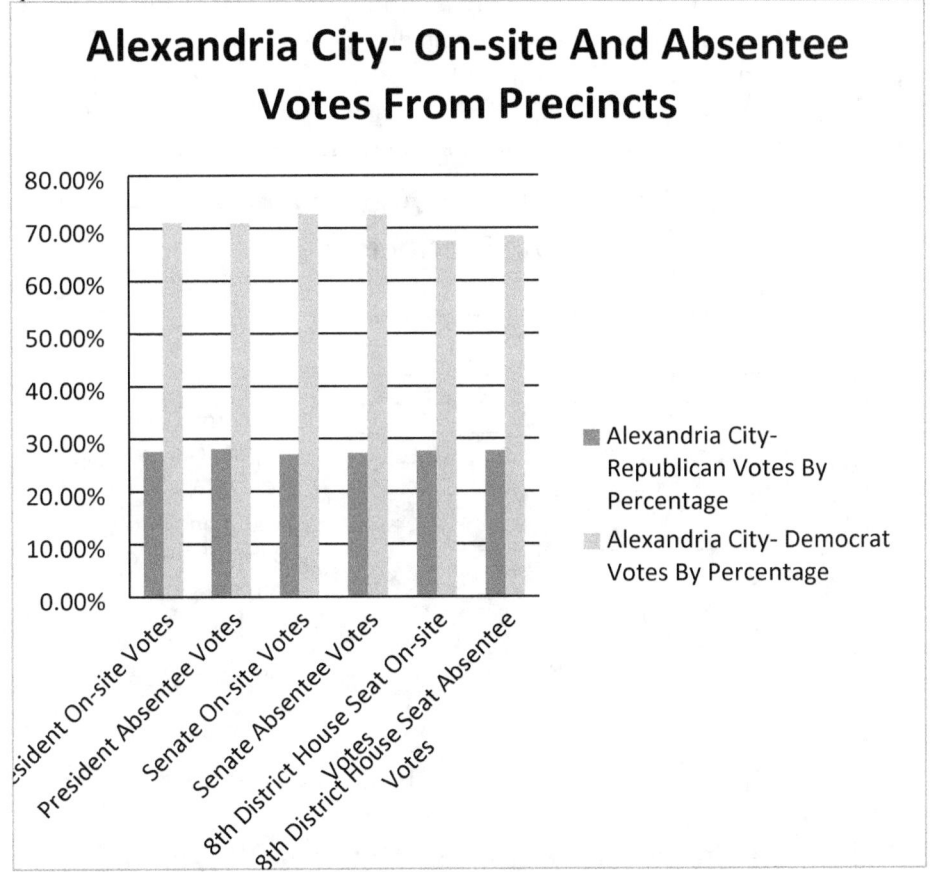

(Chart 3)

(Table 4)

Alexandria City Vote Spread Between President, Senate and House Seats On-site and Absentee

President%	Absentee%	Spread On-Site from Absentee
R) 27.58	28.06	+ .05
D) 71.10	70.91	- .13
US Senate%		
R) 27.02	27.24	+ .22
D) 72.77	72.59	- .18
8th District House%		
R) 27.61	27.70	+ .09
D) 67.50	68.56	+ 1.06

All of the spread percentages from the City of Alexandria look to follow into what most people consider to be normal. The only anomaly comes from the total percentage of Absentee votes from (Table 3), which is 21.97%. The voting characteristics do follow a logical pattern of party affiliation. A smaller sample of fraudulent votes

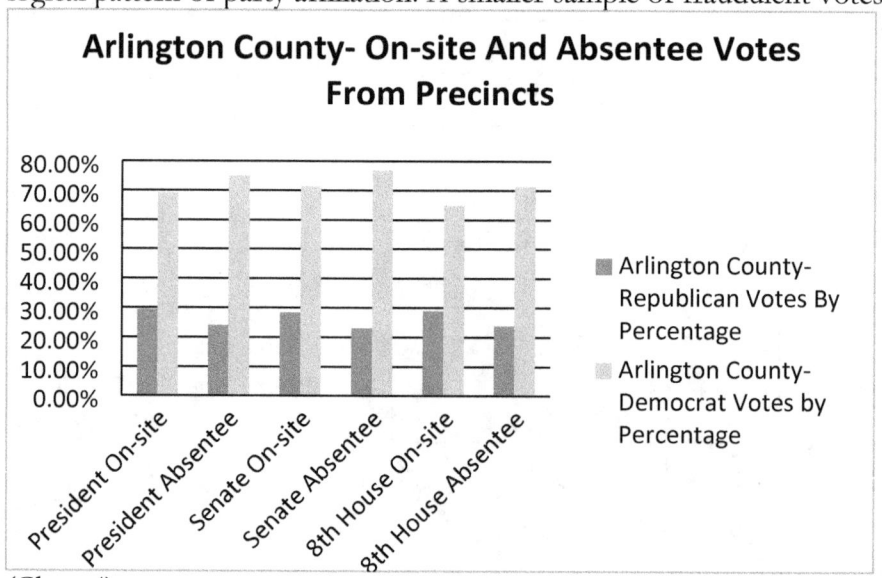

(Chart 4)

Can be easier to configure to appear to be normal.

(Table 5)

Arlington County Vote Spread Between President, Senate and House Seats On-site and Absentee

President%   Absentee%   Spread On-Site from Absentee

R) 29.31	24.00	- 5.31
D) 69.10	74.95	+ 5.85
US Senate%		
R) 28.33	23.03	- 5.3
D) 71.42	76.81	+ 5.9
8th District House%		
R) 28.93	23.73	- 5.2
D) 64.84	71.37	+ 6.53

The spread of percentages from Arlington County are where we first start to see the disturbing trend begin of what looks to be Election Fraud by itself or with institutionalized Voter Fraud, which is the hybrid I spoke to previously.

The spread in the Presidential Absentee votes gives the Democrat an 11.16% larger advantage than the Republican from the On-site figures. The spread in the Senatorial race gives the Democrat an 11.20% Absentee advantage over the Republican from the On-site figures. The spread for the 8th House Seat gives the Democrat an 11.73% Absentee advantage over the Republican from the On-site figures.

Arlington County is the second highest percentage of Absentee votes in the 8th district and by my count, the highest number of absentee votes of any single district inside of a jurisdiction in the Commonwealth of Virginia.

The anomalies I would look at are unusual vote spreads between the on-site votes and the absentee votes, which all favor the Democrat candidates and the unusual lack of variance between the amount of the spreads. It is very nearly linear from 11.16% to 11.73%. I would also add the incredibly high number of Absentee ballots at 24.62% as suspicious.

The next jurisdiction in the list of 8th District is the largest single county and is separated into three districts. The shame of this is the apparent dissolution of the idea that local governments are directly accountable to the people they serve. Those local governing bodies should be able to solicit their state and federal representatives on behalf of their constituents. Instead, after the Constitution was ratified in 1789, that theory was reversed. Many will disagree with that statement but I only have to point to the fact that according to the CDC, over 55 million babies have been aborted since abortion was legalized by a court case and not a referendum of the plebiscite. Hence, the command of the Congress to force "Southern states" to chop up their jurisdictions according to race per the Voting Rights Act, rather than allow them to represent communities according to their common interests as it was outlined in the Declaration of Rights is not to be questioned by "we the people". I have introduced my opinion here for people around the nation, who may not understand how a county could be divided up in such a manner.

In this review of data, I decided to pit the individual precinct Absentee percentages against the Total Vote mean average. I found this should identify commonality across the county if fraud is to be suspected or bolster my theory that neighborhoods, which boarder each other and share school districts or local and state representatives cannot possibly divide their loyalty of a person over their party's.

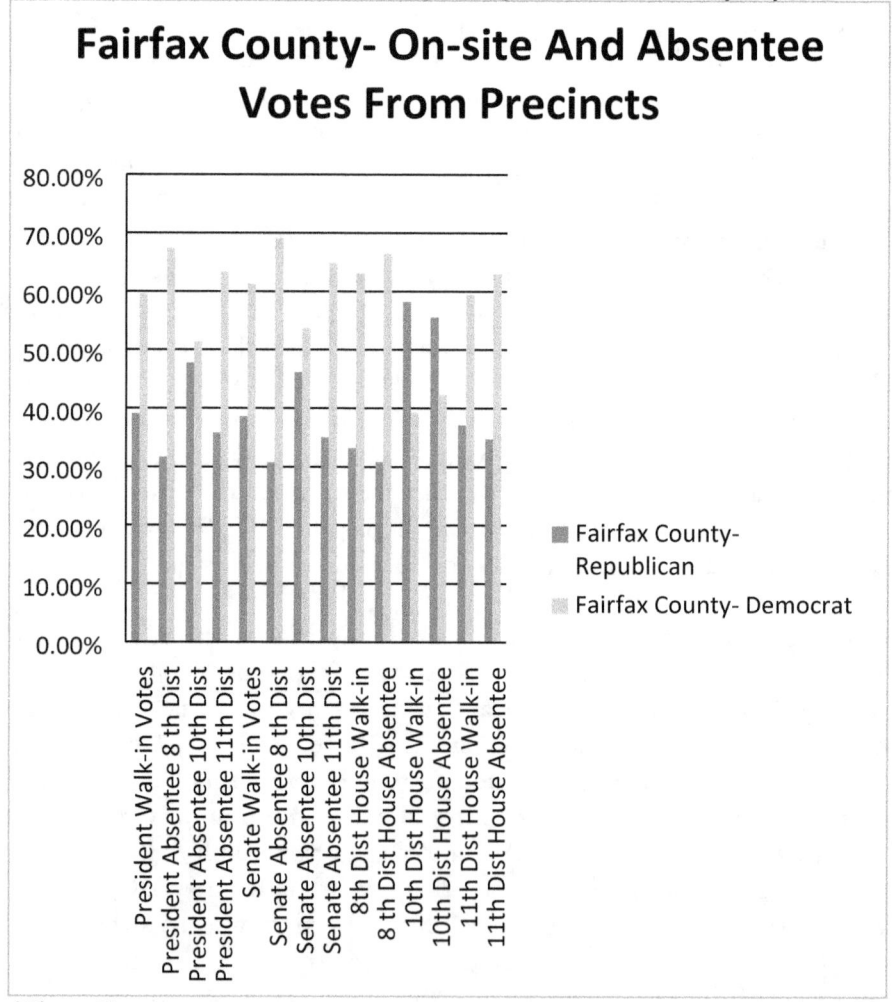

(Chart 5)

(Table 6)

Fairfax County Vote Spread Between President, Senate and House Seats On-site and Absentee

President%	Absentee%		Spread On-Site from Absentee
R) 39.06	8th	31.66	- 7.4
D) 59.56		67.36	+ 7.8
	10th	47.74	+ 8.68
		51.39	- 8.17
	11th	35.78	- 3.28
		63.29	+ 3.73
US Senate%			
R) 38.56	8th	30.73	- 7.83
D) 61.21		69.01	+ 7.80
	10th	46.13	+ 7.57
		53.73	- 7.48
	11th	34.99	- 3.57
		64.87	+ 3.66
8th District House%			
R) 33.17		30.76	- 2.41
D) 63.04		66.43	+ 3.39
10th District House%			
R) 58.20		55.56	- 2.64
D) 39.28		42.33	+ 3.05
11th District House%			
R) 37.11		34.71	- 2.40
D) 59.44		62.96	+ 3.52

The spread of percentages from Fairfax County, mirror that of Arlington County with one exception in the Congressional House race of the 10th District. This is yet another disturbing anomaly, which proved my suspicion of splitting neighborhood voting lines and coming up with a dramatic difference in candidate performance versus party affiliation of the adjoining neighborhoods.

The spread in each of the races are broken down by Congressional district performance from the total average performance of the county On-site totals. The percentages for a direct comparison were not published by the VBOE at the time of my queries for information.

The Presidential Absentee spread from the 8th was 15.2% in favor of the Democrat from On-site total average. The 10th was 16.5% in favor of the Democrat. The 11th was 7.01% in favor of the Democrat from the On-site total average.

The Senatorial Absentee spread from the 8th was 15.63% in favor of the Democrat difference over the On-site average. The 10th was a 15.05% spread in favor of the Democrat over the On-site average. The 11th District was 7.23% in favor of the Democrat from the spread out of the On-site average.

The House race of the 8th, a 5.8% spread in favor of the Democrat over the On-site spread. The House race in the 10th, has a spread of 5.69% in favor of the Republican over the On-site averages. The House race of the 11th, shows a 5.92% spread in favor of the Democrat over the On-site votes.

Outside of the unusually high number of absentee votes (by my count the 2nd highest in the 8th District and the highest of any place in the Commonwealth when combining all the districts in the county), which is an anomaly in itself, you will notice the 10th District House race performance is radically different from the other two House races, which bracket the 10th on either side in the same county. It differs in that it went for the Republican House candidate and its On-site percentage spread was almost identical for the Republican as was the spread for the two Democrats who bracketed that district. However, the absentee spread average for the Republican decreased in a near identical percentage as with the other house races and the Democrat percentage increased in a near identical fashion to the other races. It was still not enough to garner a victory for the Democrat challenger.

Another anomaly is the comparing of the performance in the 10th District votes for President and Senator. In the Presidential Absentee spread, we see the 10th District voting is the highest in the county between the other two districts.

In the Senate race, the 10th comes in a near second place finish by a fraction to the 8th District in the Absentee spread.

The larger question is, how can this section of a county vote so opposite their immediate neighbors in such landslide proportions? They share the same water, real estate, schools, places of worship, shopping centers, many career occupations and most likely the same political views. How can they have such a split for a party and a candidate whose primary constituency lives far away from them and have little in common with each other,? It is a big question and as we move forward, it may get bigger and the obvious answer may not be a warm and fuzzy one.

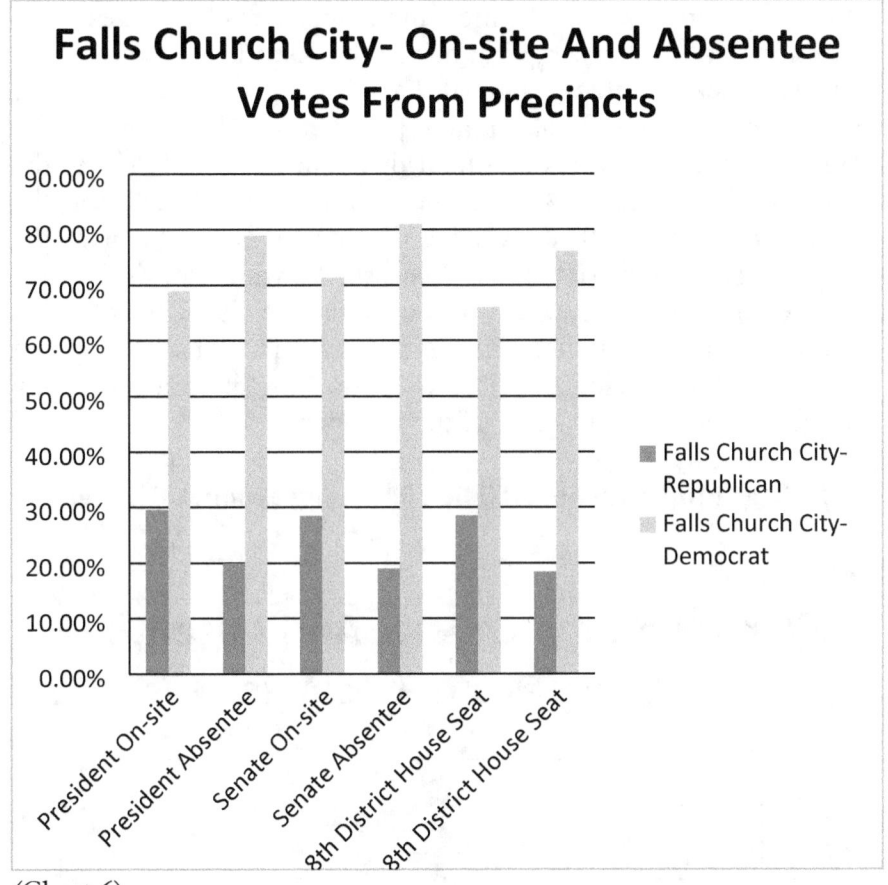

(Chart 6)

(Table 7)

Falls Church City Vote Spread Between President, Senate and House Seats On-site and Absentee

President%	Absentee%	Spread On-Site from Absentee
R) 29.50	19.94	- 9.56
D) 68.92	78.86	+ 9.94
US Senate%		
R) 28.44	18.95	- 9.49
D) 71.37	80.95	+ 9.58

8th District House%

R) 28.49	18.37	- 10.12
D) 66.04	76.11	+10.07

In Falls Church, we see the most incredible spread averages I was able to find in all of the sampling of districts used in this study. The anomalies stack up this way. It has the highest percentage of absentee votes in the state of any jurisdiction. The spread for Presidential Absentee votes is a total difference of 19.55% over the On-site figures in favor of the Democrat. The spread for the Senatorial race was 19.07% over the On-site figures in favor of the Democrat. The 8th District House race was the winner of the highest ratio difference from Absentee Votes from the On-site figures I could find in all of the jurisdictions in this survey. The Absentee spread came in at a whopping 20.19% over the On-site Election Day performance and it was in favor of the Democrat.

Moving Into Elements Of The 10th Congressional District

(Chart 7)

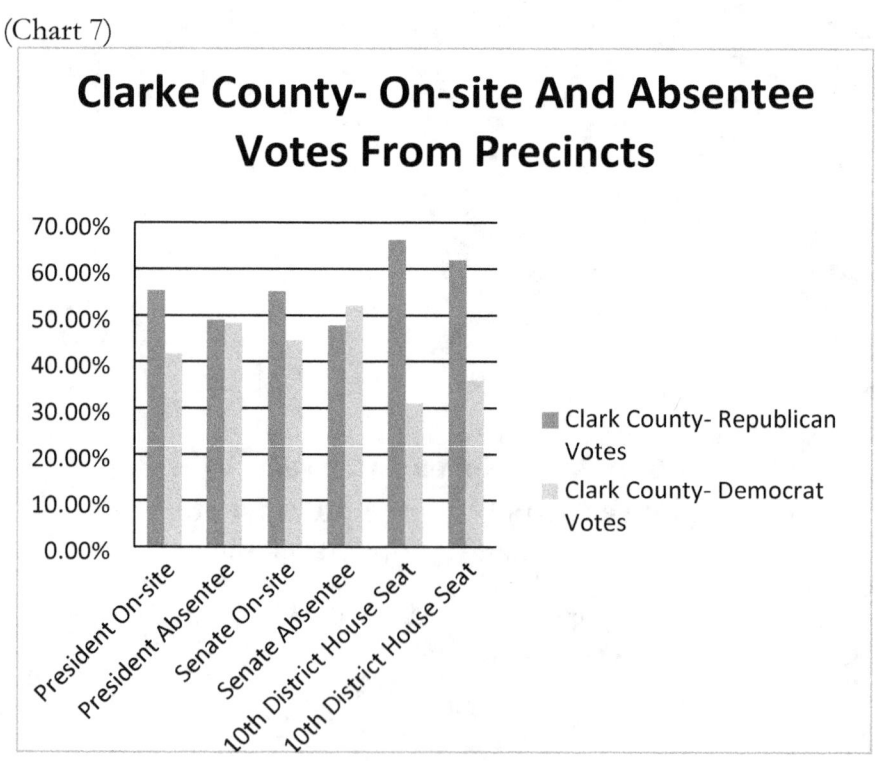

(Table 8)

Clarke County Vote Spread Between President, Senate and House Seats On-site and Absentee

President%	Absentee%	Spread On-Site from Absentee
R) 55.34	48.99	- 6.35
D) 41.72	48.36	+ 6.64
US Senate%		
R) 55.15	47.77	- 7.38
D) 44.64	52.10	+ 7.46
10th District House%		
R) 66.23	61.87	- 4.36
D) 30.97	35.90	+4.93

Table 7 shows an incredible phenomenon in the On-site percentage of the spread of votes (13.62%) by the winner in the Presidential race for this county was almost all but erased by a 12.99% reversal in the performance of the returns in the Absentee ballots.

In the US Senate race, a shocking reversal takes place. The On-site percentage landside style victory for the Republican was reversed in the Absentee ballots to a landslide victory for the Democrat. The vote spread in the Absentee ballot difference was 14.84% from the On-site percentages with a complete reversal of winner to loser with an identical ratio.

Here we are again, looking into the 10th District House seat. The same seat shared with parts of Fairfax County and is an entire county away. It is in the heart of the 10th District and has a slightly larger percentage of On-site performance in favor of the <u>Republican.</u> The total spread was 9.29% and as has been the case for all of the jurisdictions, the absentee difference favors into the Democrat Party in all races and this ratio is almost the exact same to Fairfax County.

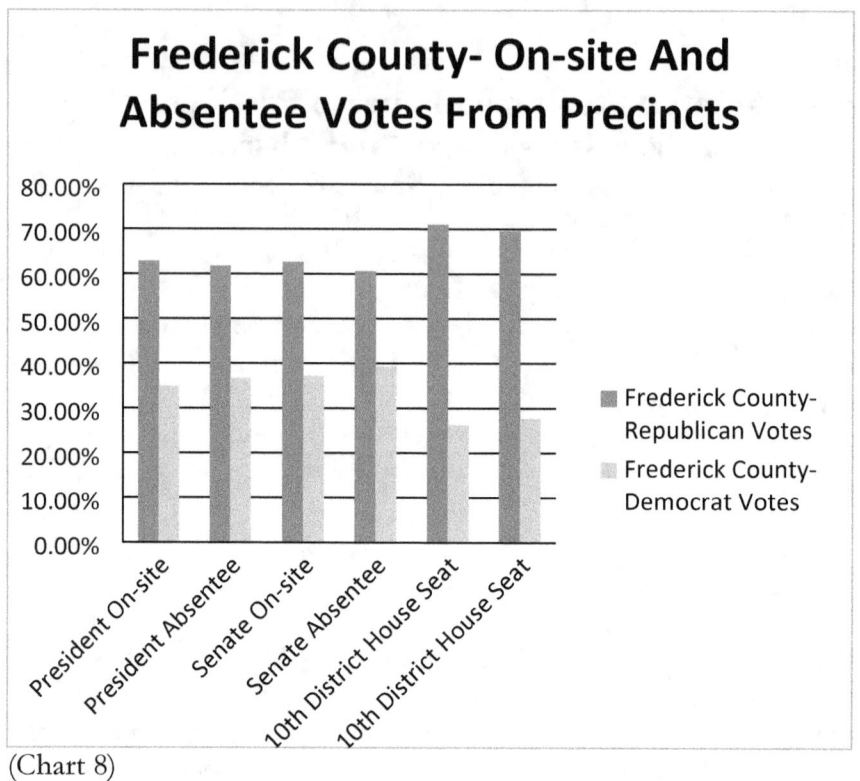

Frederick County- On-site And Absentee Votes From Precincts

Legend:
- Frederick County- Republican Votes
- Frederick County- Democrat Votes

Categories: President On-site, President Absentee, Senate On-site, Senate Absentee, 10th District House Seat, 10th District House Seat

(Chart 8)

(Table 9)

Frederick County Vote Spread Between President, Senate and House Seats On-site and Absentee

President%	Absentee%	Spread On-Site from Absentee
R) 62.80	61.72	- 1.08
D) 34.86	36.64	+ 1.78
US Senate%		
R) 62.62	60.55	- 2.07
D) 37.19	39.28	+ 2.09
10th District House%		
R) 70.94	69.52	- 1.42
D) 26.30	27.75	+1.45

Here in Frederick County, we instantly see at a glance that the a pattern of Absentee vote percentage reversal in favor of the Democrats takes place. The spread from the Presidential race is 2.86 % more Absentee votes going to the Democrat.

The US Senate race shows the same pattern. In the Absentee ballots, the Republican lost 2.07% from the On-site voting and the Democrat gained 2.09% of the Absentee ballots giving the Democrat the spread of 4.16% over the performance of the On-site Votes.

As with Clarke County, Frederick has its largely rural districts around places such as Winchester City and Stephens City. This has been traditionally conservative and, yet, we see the identical ratio pattern, which matches the other races in the county of taking away percentages of votes from Republicans and adding votes to Democrats. The total reversal of the winning Absentee ballot count shows a spread of 3.87%. It takes 1.42% away from the Republican and adds 1.45% to the Democrat. Again and interestingly, this takes place in the face of a jurisdiction wide Republican On-site landslide.

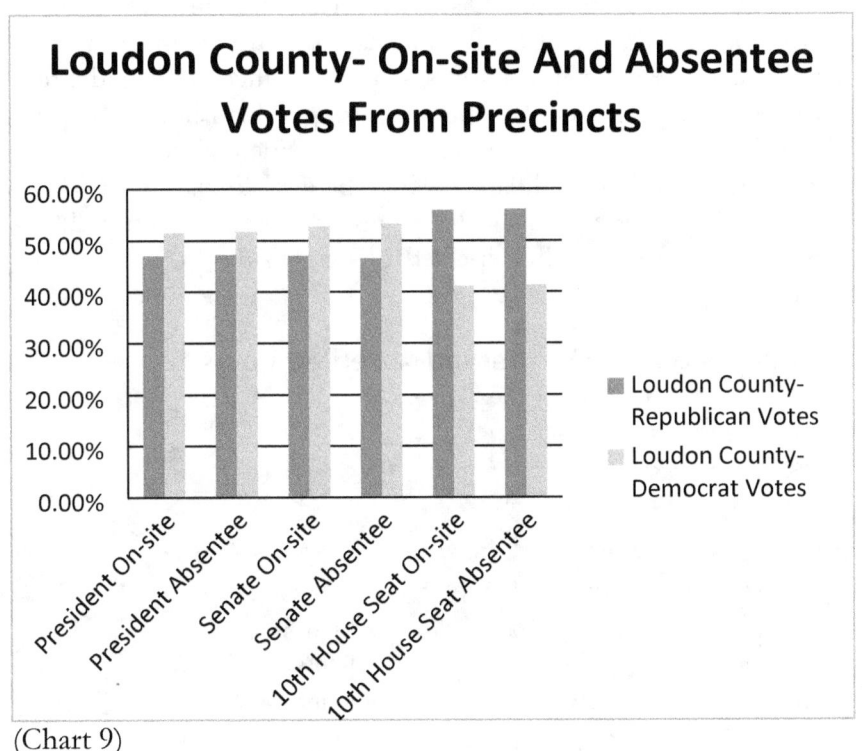

(Chart 9)

(Table 10)

Loudon County Vote Spread Between President, Senate and House Seats On-site and Absentee

President%	Absentee%	Spread On-Site from Absentee
R) 47.03	47.19	+ .16

D) 51.53   51.72   + .19
US Senate%
R) 47.04   46.54   - .5
D) 52.78   53.28   + .5
10th District House%
R) 55.86   56.05   + .19
D) 41.06   41.28   + .22

In what appears to be the most believable performance in a Northern jurisdiction when it comes to Absentee ratios deviating from the On-site performance, Loudoun County looks to be stable and more of a baseline for absentee performance. The ratios are all under one percent and that is what you would expect from your demographics.

It is worth noting in the 10th District House race, the percentage of winner over loser in favor of the Republican is nearly identical with its Fairfax County Counterpart in On-site performance. This identical pattern of the 10th District Republican getting a landslide in another jurisdiction, which voted for the Democrat Presidential candidate and the Democrat Senatorial candidate needs to be explained.

Loudoun County does show a slight sign of higher than normal On-site voting percentage over the expected Absentee side. (Chart 10)

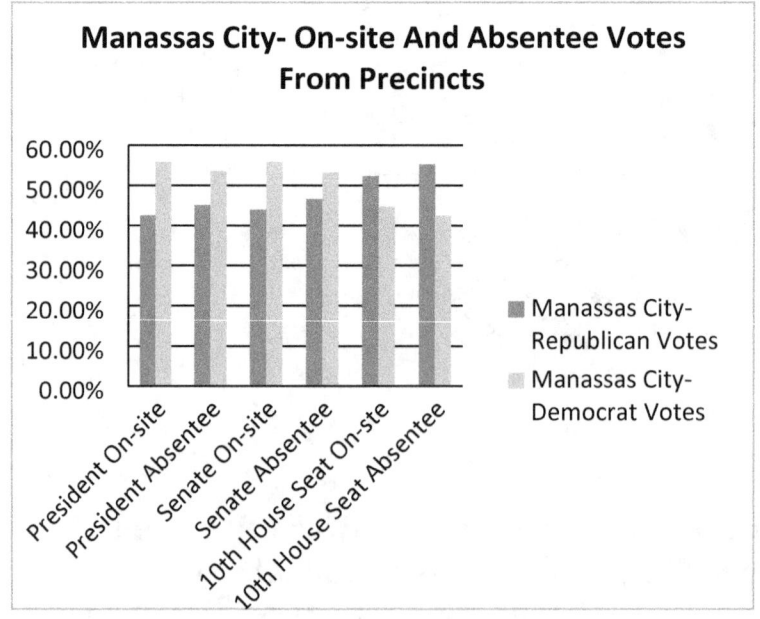

(Table 11)
Manassas City Vote Spread Between President, Senate and House Seats On-site and Absentee

President%	Absentee%	Spread On-Site from Absentee
R) 42.51	45.11	+ 2.6
D) 55.77	53.60	-2.17
US Senate%		
R) 43.96	46.63	+ 2.67
D) 55.85	53.25	- 2.6
10th District House%		
R) 52.30	55.21	+ 2.91
D) 44.67	42.56	- 2.11

In Manassas City, we see a scenario that is opposite from the results of the vast majority of the other jurisdictions in this study. It is as if this were a murder trial where the person indicted for the crime is found innocent and the real killer is paraded on the witness stand to blow the case and the trial wide open.

Little Manassas City is such a place. The Absentee spreads work completely against the Democrats and for the Republicans and is the opposite for On-site results. The Democrats would say that is a "got you" moment and it blows the whole thesis out of the water. Sorry, just the opposite is true in my opinion.

When we see the momentum of the vastly larger On-site voting in the opposite of the static inventory of Absentee votes and using Counties such as Loudoun as the base line for normality in election results, then you see evidence of On-site voter fraud. Rare as this might seem to be, it is proven to take place. In this instance, the Absentee spread for the President favors the Republican by 4.77% over the Democrat compared to the percentage of the On-site tallies. The US Senate at 5.27% to the Republican and that ever-interesting 10th House Seat coming in at 3.02% Republican favored over the Democrat in the ratio versus the On-site total.

Manassas City has demographics very similar to the makeup of Fairfax County and yet the 10th District House race came in weaker than its Fairfax County counterpart. The Absentee results from Manassas City are within one-half of one percent of the Fairfax County tallies.

This spells the culprit here to be On-site voter fraud and quite a bit of it to make up that kind of percentage and proving it is a bit in the reverse of what we have been looking at in the line for line difference between the Absentee percentages and the On-site results.

First, we can take the total votes from Manassas City for the presidential race. This gives us 14,941 per my calculations. Then we take the percentage represented by the Absentee results (45.11 for the Republican) and take that amount from 14,941 votes, we will see the Republican's vote total increase by 277 votes to 6,740 as opposed to the published number from the On-site total of 6,463.

Because we are dealing with only two percentages to compare, and there was an increase in the Republican's expected vote total, we can expect the decrease in the Democrat's vote total to be equal in size of 277 votes. This can be proven by handling the equation on the other side by taking the Absentee percentage of the Democrat (53.60) and taking it from the number of total votes 14,941 you find it yields 8,201, which is 277 votes fewer than the On-site results.

I could not say that exactly 554 illegal votes were cast in favor of the Democrat; however, it does point in that direction against the comparison with the base line performances of other jurisdictions. The new vote totals would have been the Republican 6,740 versus the Democrat 8,201.

In a "Voter Fraud" operation, 554 votes may appear to be a large number; however, it is not that far-fetched and would only need something around 140 different people, lined up with six different identities to commit this type of Voter Fraud in Manassas City. This is because Manassas City has six precincts and one is Absentee and the other Considered Provisional. You could have teams of about 30 to 35 people travel around in buses or vans all day and get them to vote.

(Chart 11)

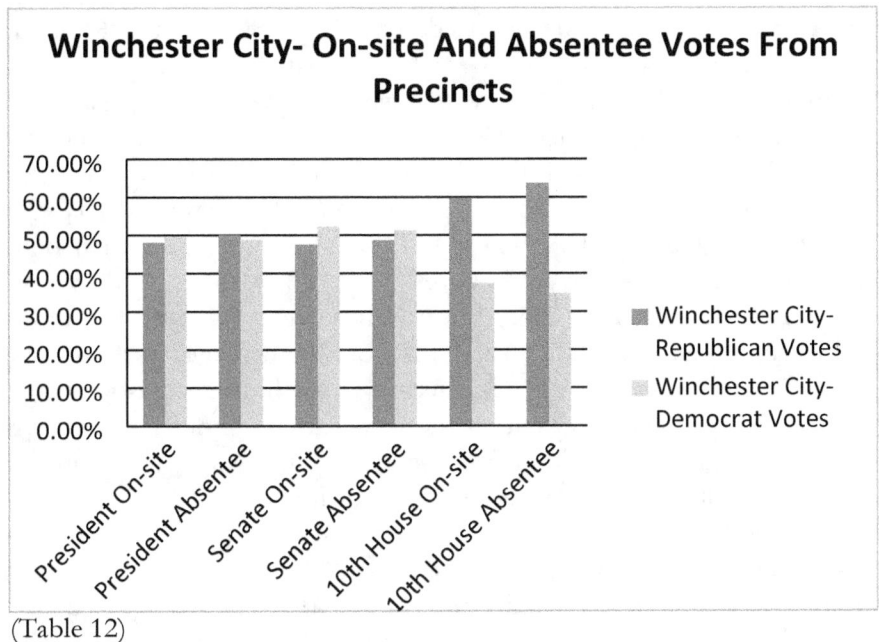

(Table 12)

Winchester City Vote Spread Between President, Senate and House Seats On-site and Absentee

President%	Absentee%	Spread On-Site from Absentee
R) 48.03	50.04	+ 2.01
D) 49.47	48.81	- 0.66
US Senate%		
R) 47.50	46.63	- 0.87
D) 52.20	53.25	+ 1.05
10th District House%		
R) 59.81	63.62	+ 3.81
D) 37.46	34.77	-02.69

Curiously, this small independent city of Winchester shows a similar reverse scenario found in the analysis of Manassas City. The momentum of the On-site votes breaks away from the pattern of the static Absentee ballots. This supports the notion of On-site fraud on Election Day. All of the races covered here, show a momentum to the Democrat. We can apply the same method of seeking a percentage on what we would expect to have in the light of the base line of Loudoun County's results and, which we used in the investigation of Manassas City's numbers.

Taking only the total of Presidential votes cast for the Republican and the Democrat, we have a total of 10,040 from the full-published number of 10,296. Taking the published Absentee percentage of the Republican (50.40) from 10,040 gives us 5,060 votes and the remainder in the Democrat side of 4,980. Going to double check this, we take the published Democrat Absentee percentage (48.81) from the 10,040 and we find the Democrat getting 4,900 votes (80 votes less than before) and the Republican with 5,140 votes.

This should have worked out exactly in reverse and it did not. In addition, please note, I referred to those percentages as "published" and they are or were. A quick check against the Manassas City figures shows that more votes went to the three other candidates and "write-in" column than went to the Democrat in Winchester. That comes out to a 0.79% difference between the two equations.

This leaves us with a potential difference from the On-site results in using the Absentee percentages as "norm" to these approximates: The Republican would have had 5,060 or 5,140 votes as opposed to the published 4,946 from the On-site results. The Democrat would have had 4,980 or 4,900 votes as opposed to the published of 5,094 On-site results. In either case, the published winner of the contest would have been overturned and the Republican would have been the winner had the On-site performance been within expected norms.

Using the same theory, the US Senate contest sees an interesting higher count of total votes over that of the Presidential column. This further confirms more votes going to other Presidential candidates in a race of more than two candidates. The Senate total votes are 10,108 and using the (48.58%), published Absentee votes for the Republican, we would have expected a return of 4,910 votes, which is 94 votes more than the published 4,816. That left a balance of 5,198 votes for the Democrat, which are 94 votes less than the published 5,292 votes.

More curiously is the never disappointing wonder of the 10th District House race. In the face of the two top ticket races running very close to each other, the Republican comes in with another landslide. Yet, like the other two top races on the ticket, the Republican has noticeably lower momentum in the On-site vote ratio as opposed to those in the Absentee results. The momentum is for the Democrat by comparison; however, it was not enough to come for a race reversal, as has been the case for all of the other jurisdictions, which host the 10th District House race.

In the comparison of the House race, using the Absentee model again to derive a number of votes by percentage from the separated total vote number (those which were cast for Democrat and Republican only, which is 9,437) we see the expected result comes to us in two different ratios. The percentages given to us come from the VBOE and came from no other source. The Republican, using the published (63.62%) of the absentee figure as a base line of performance, gives us 6,004 votes from the total 9,437 votes. That would be 203 more votes to the Republican. It would leave us with 3,433 votes for the Democrat and 201 votes less than the published 3,634 votes. It is a total of 404 votes for a spread, which continues to show a momentum on the street over the static absentee votes.

Using the published Democrat Absentee number as the origin of the percentage of the total number, you would take (34.77%) from the total of 9,437 and get 3,281 votes for the Democrat. That makes for an even larger spread at 353 less votes for the Democrat. This would leave 6,156 votes for the Republican margin. That gives us 356 more votes than the published figures for the On-site tally. It is a spread of 709 votes. It is very possible for 356 to 709 votes to be cast by a team of fraud voters during an election day.

Wrapping up Elements of the 10th District and Closing With The Elements of the 11th District

(Chart 12)

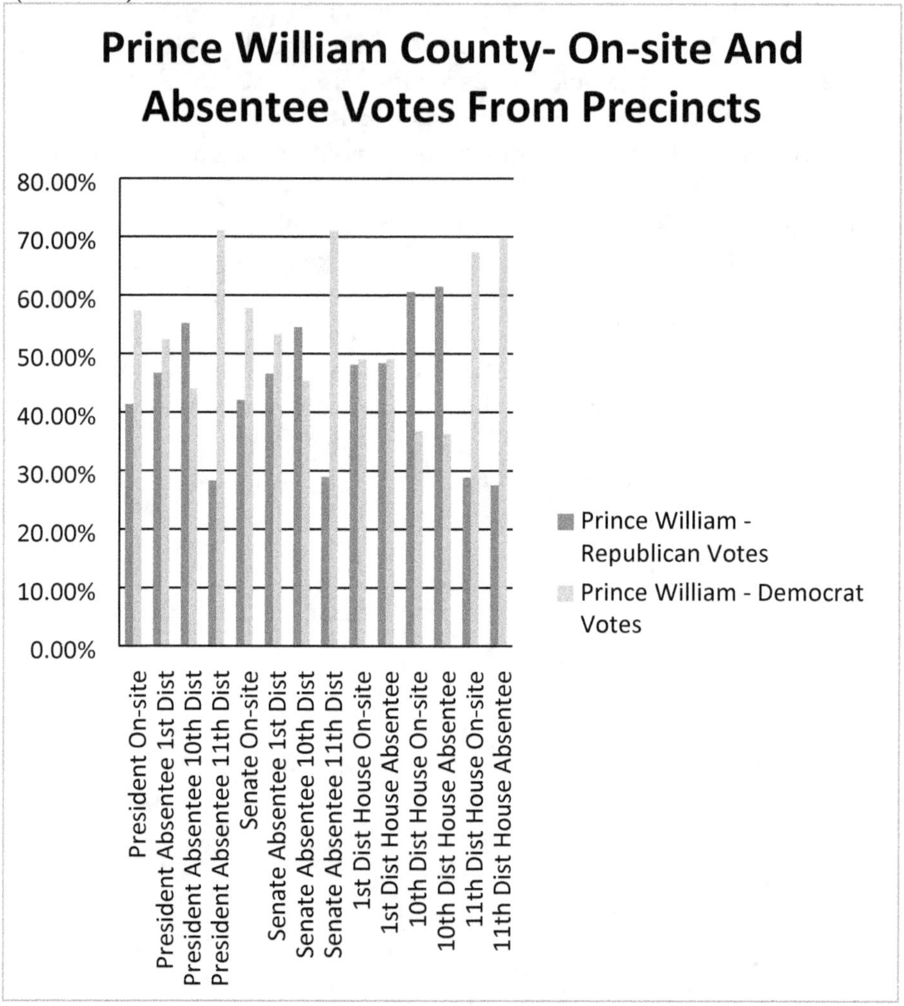

Prince William County- On-site And Absentee Votes From Precincts
80.00%
70.00%
60.00%
50.00%
40.00%
30.00%
20.00%
10.00%
0.00%
President On-site
President Absentee 1st Dist
President Absentee 10th Dist
President Absentee 11th Dist
Senate On-site
Senate Absentee 1st Dist
Senate Absentee 10th Dist
Senate Absentee 11th Dist
1st Dist House On-site
1st Dist House Absentee
10th Dist House On-site
10th Dist House Absentee
11th Dist House On-site
11th Dist House Absentee
Prince William - Republican Votes
Prince William - Democrat Votes

(Table 13)

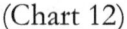

Prince William County Vote Spread Between President, Senate and House Seats On-site and Absentee

President%	Absentee%	Spread On-Site from Absentee
R) 41.32	1st 46.67	+5.35
D) 57.34	52.36	-4.98
	10th 55.21	+ 13.89
	44.02	- 13.32
	11th 28.23	- 13.09
	71.10	+ 13.76
US Senate%		
R) 38.56	1st 46.56	+ 8.0
D) 61.21	53.32	-7.89
	10th 54.59	+ 16.03
	45.36	- 15.85
	11th 28.91	- 9.65
	70.98	+ 9.77
1st District House%		
R) 33.17	48.35	+ 15.18
D) 63.04	49.10	- 13.94
10th District House%		
R) 58.20	61.50	+ 3.3
D) 39.28	36.28	- 3.0
11th District House%		
R) 37.11	27.48	- 9.63
D) 59.44	69.64	+ 10.20

It is with great regret that I take on the task of analyzing the Prince William County voting results. Prince William County is the bottom of the 10th and 11th Congressional Districts and it is the very top of the 1st Congressional district, which extends approximately 180 miles southward to and including some of the city of Newport News, VA. It is like Fairfax County in that it has three separate districts running through it. Prince William County has as diverse a mix of topography and demography that you will find in Virginia. It also encompasses the famous Quantico Marine Base at the top of its First District.

Sadly, it is my opinion that after reviewing the Absentee performance against the On-site voting patterns in Prince William County, I can only conclude that it suffers from massive Election Fraud, Voter Fraud, and what I call Mechanical System Election Fraud.

I see it taken down and manipulated. It leads me to believe the voting results presented to us by the Government cannot possibly be correct.

The Presidential race spread calculation is again like Fairfax, not a direct district percentage to district percentage. Those exact breakdowns with the jurisdictions were not available as a ready tabulated figure. Perhaps the new website will break that down further. It does however give a view as to how each District's pattern works against the mean average of the entire jurisdiction.

The Republican's Presidential candidate had a 5.35% more Absentee performance in the 1st District over the On-site results. The Republican had a 13.89% higher Absentee performance in the 10th District than the On-site results. The Republican had a 13.09% lower Absentee performance in the 11th District than the On-site results.

The Democrat's Presidential candidate had a 4.98% lower Absentee performance in the 1st than the On-site results. The Democrat had a 13.32% lower Absentee Performance in the 10th District than the On-site results. The Democrat had a 13.76% higher Absentee performance in the 11th District than the On-site results.

By using the discovery method from Manassas City and Winchester City, I can see evidence, which makes me suspect On-site Voter Fraud taking place in the 1st and 10th District precincts because the Republican On-site average is more than 2 percentage points lower than the Absentee results. The ever-interesting 10th District appears to have landslide proportions for the Republican Candidate. Here is where I suspect a Mechanical System type of Fraud as this is a scenario, which has repeated across numerous Communities in the 10th District and is bracketed by strong opposition. I suspect this type of fraud takes place after the actual voting results leave the precincts and could be manipulated by those who handle the results. They can change them in complete secrecy and then send them back into the country. The results from the 11th District show strong possible Absentee fraud.

The Republican Senate candidate had an 8.0% higher Absentee average in the 1st District over the On-site performance. The Republican had a 16.03% higher Absentee average in the 10th district than the On-site results. The Republican had a 9.65% lower Absentee average in the 11th District than the On-site Average.

The Democrat had a 7.89% lower Absentee average in the 1st District than the On-site performance. The Democrat had a 15.85% lower performance in the 10th District than the On-site performance. The Democrat had 9.77% higher Absentee average in the 11th District over the On-site performance.

Again, the performance of the Districts and their Absentee percentages as a base line, leave us in turmoil. The 1st and 10th districts suffer from possible On-site voter fraud. The 11th District looks to be suffering from massive Absentee Fraud. Again, there appears to be a guardian angel for Republicans in the 10th District Absentee tallies.

The house races can be broken down directly. The 1st District House race shows strong evidence of On-site Voter Fraud. The Republican had a 15.18% higher Absentee performance than the On-site performance. The Democrat had a 13.94% lower Absentee performance than the On-site performance. That is a spread of 29.12% in the change of the Absentee performance over the On-site results.

The 10th District House looks to suffer from similar On-site fraud but suspiciously, when it goes bad for this District House seat, it is not that bad. It is not as bad as it is for the other offices in the 8th and 11th District sections of the County. The Republican was 3.3% higher in the Absentee percentage over the On-site performance. The Democrat had a 3.0% lower Absentee percentage than the On-site performance. It gives us a spread of 6.3%. The 11th District again sees the possibility of massive Absentee Fraud. The Republican had a 9.63% lower Absentee percentage than the On-site results. The Democrat had a 10.20% higher Absentee average over the On-site.

I would sum it up as the 1st and 10th Districts suffered harshly from On-site (Walk in with a fake ID) voter fraud. The 11th District suffered harshly from Absentee Ballot fraud (dead people, non-citizens, dual registered, etc.). Then there is this guardian angel over the 10th district seat, which makes sure it is an island of safety for the Republican candidate.

Some would point their finger at the redistricting process; however, I would not. There is no way communities such as Fairfax County and Prince William could carry such difference from one neighborhood to another because for the most part, they are all the same demographically speaking. I suspect manipulation mechanically or electronically, after the votes had been cast or pre-programmed in the processing of the votes. This is a charge often referred to as "Vote Weighting".

Before you the reader start having doubts about On-site Voter Fraud, remember that the City of Manassas, sits squarely inside the County of Prince William and we have already seen those results. This is why I regret having to show what I have found. I know Prince William to have very friendly and good people living in it. It is a shame there appears to be a politically criminal element within it.

(Chart 13)

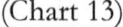

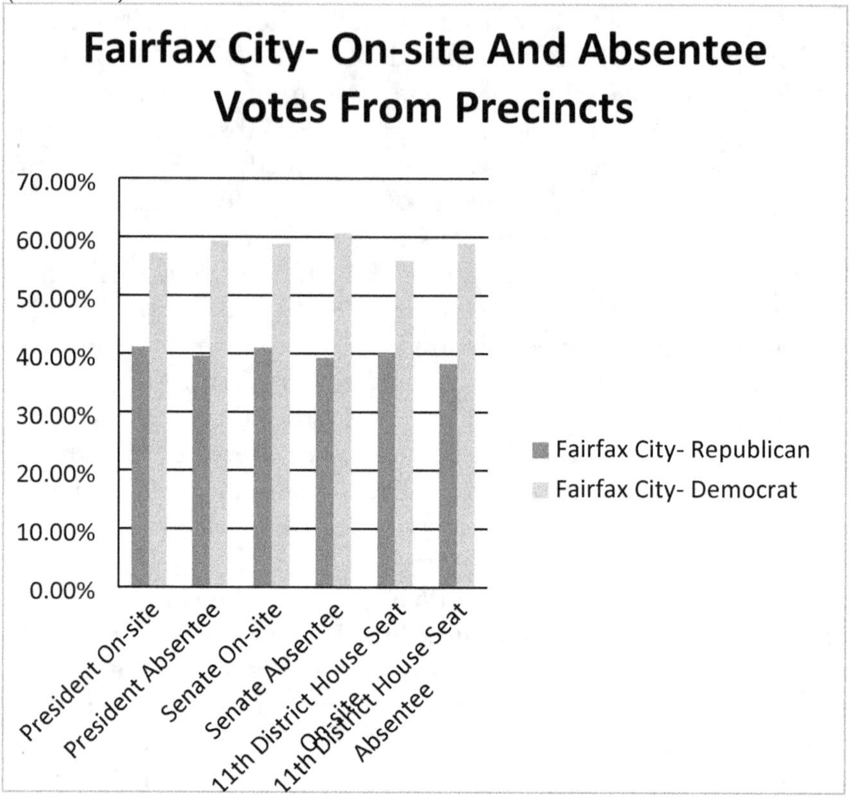

Fairfax City- On-site And Absentee Votes From Precincts

Legend:
- Fairfax City- Republican
- Fairfax City- Democrat

(Table 14)

Fairfax City Vote Spread Between President, Senate and House Seats On-site and Absentee

President%	Absentee%	Spread On-Site from Absentee
R) 41.06	39.49	- 1.57
D) 57.19	59.29	+ 2.10
US Senate%		
R) 40.94	39.26	- 1.68
D) 58.83	60.61	+ 1.78
11th District House%		
R) 40.09	38.28	-1.81
D) 55.90	58.93	+3.03

I do not want to brush this jurisdiction aside for convenience sake. However, if you've not gotten lost in the crazy results from the previous jurisdictional breakdowns, you will see by Table 14, the only thing, which would raise your attention at a glance would be the narrow ratios between Absentee percentages and On-site percentages

If I had to judge if there was fraud involved, I would say it existed in the Absentee votes. The percentage is above my 2% threshold for suspicion in the vote spreads. In a jurisdiction of this size, the percentage of fraud would have to be kept low due to its ability to stick out of the ordinary at a glance.

The fraud does not help the winner over the finish line; however, it does help in the overall vote total across the state in similar instances.

3 ELEMENTS OF THE RURAL WESTERN SECTION

(Chart 14)

Fauquier County- On-site And Absentee Votes From Precincts

Legend:
- Fauquier County- Republican Votes
- Fauquier County- Democrat Votes

(Table 15)

Fauquier County Vote Spread Between President, Senate and House Seats On-site and Absentee

President%		Absentee%	Spread On-Site from Absentee
R) 59.15	1st	62.87	+3.72
D) 39.27		35.64	- 3.63
	5th	58.85	-0.30
		40.02	+ 0.75

US Senate%		Absentee%	
R) 58.99	1st	62.72	+3.73
D) 40.81		37.02	-3.79
	5th	57.77	-1.22
		42.09	+1.28

1st District House%			
R) 64.65		65.81	+1.16
D) 32.39		31.88	- 0.51
5th District House%			
R) 58.22		59.23	+ 1.01
D) 39.18		39.15	- 0.03

In the first of three rural counties I have chosen for the second region of comparison, it appears that the Republican Presidential candidate had a 3.72% better Absentee performance than the On-site results in the 1st District. The Democrat had a 3.63% higher On-site performance than the Absentee performance in the 1st district. This 7.35% spread and onsite figures outside of the normal expectations show a high probability of On-site Voter Fraud of the same style we have seen in the other smaller jurisdictions.

The Republican and Democrat 5th district results reflect what you would expect from the same group of voters and no fraud is apparent in the 5th district precincts

The Senatorial Republican candidate in the 1st district showed almost exactly the same results as the Presidential results. The Republican was 3.73% higher in Absentee results over the On-site performance. The Democrat was 3.79% higher in the On-site voter percentage than the Absentee performance. This gives us a spread of 7.52%. With the Democrat gaining the percentage and the Republican losing the percentage at the On-site polls, this shows again that a high possibility of On-Site (walk-in) voter fraud has occurred in the 1st District precincts.

Again, the 5th district results for US Senate mirror the acceptable margin of error you would expect in a normal election and see no evidence of foul play in the 5th District of Fauquier County.

Both the 1st and 5th District House races look to have an acceptable spread between the Absentee vote percentages and the On-site percentages.

Only the 1st District precincts appear to have On-Site voter fraud taking place. No other type of fraud looks to be taking place.

(Chart 15)

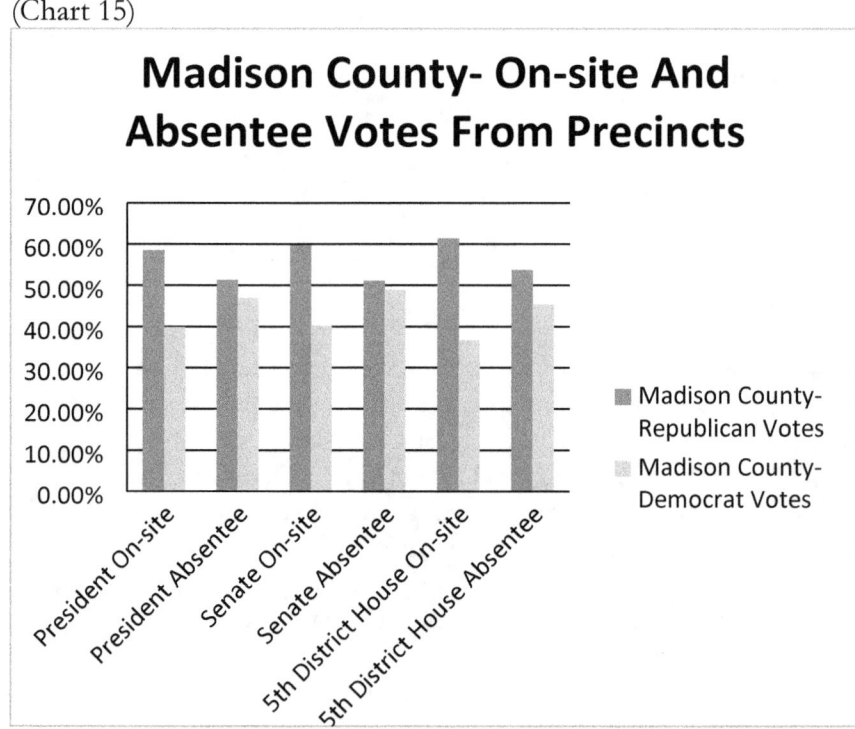

(Table 16)

Madison County Vote Spread Between President, Senate and House Seats On-site and Absentee

President%	Absentee%	Spread On-Site from Absentee
R) 58.49	51.35	- 7.14
D) 39.90	46.97	+7.07
US Senate%		
R) 59.72	51.12	- 8.60
D) 40.20	48.87	+ 8.67
5th District House%		
R) 61.34	53.70	-7.64
D) 36.67	45.37	+ 8.70

Madison County, Republican Presidential candidate had 7.14% lower Absentee results than the On-site performance. The Democrat had an increase of 7.07% of Absentee vote percentage over the On-site performance. The spread is a shocking 14.21%.

The US Senate Republican candidate was 8.60% lower in the absentee percentage than the On-site performance. The Democrat was 8.67% higher in the Absentee percentage over the On-site performance. This is a shocking 17.27% spread.

The 5th district House seat showed the Republican candidate had a negative 7.64% average of Absentee performance compared to the On-site performance. The Democrat was 8.70% higher in the Absentee results over the On-site performance. This gives us a 16.34% spread of percentage difference.

Though it did not change any of the outcomes in this jurisdiction, the Apparent Absentee fraud in situations like this one will quietly add to the bottom line of the other candidate. They are free votes. It is my opinion that although the number of Absentee votes may not be large compared to other jurisdictions, in my opinion, a large amount of Absentee Fraud taking place in Madison County.

Is it not interesting how these rural areas are mostly in the light of one political party and when the election is over, they do not think to look at the results because the results for their area went as they expected. They say, "My person won my county so what might the problem be?" The problem looks to be their opponent is stealing votes to add to their victories in the popular total elsewhere in the state.

(Chart 16)

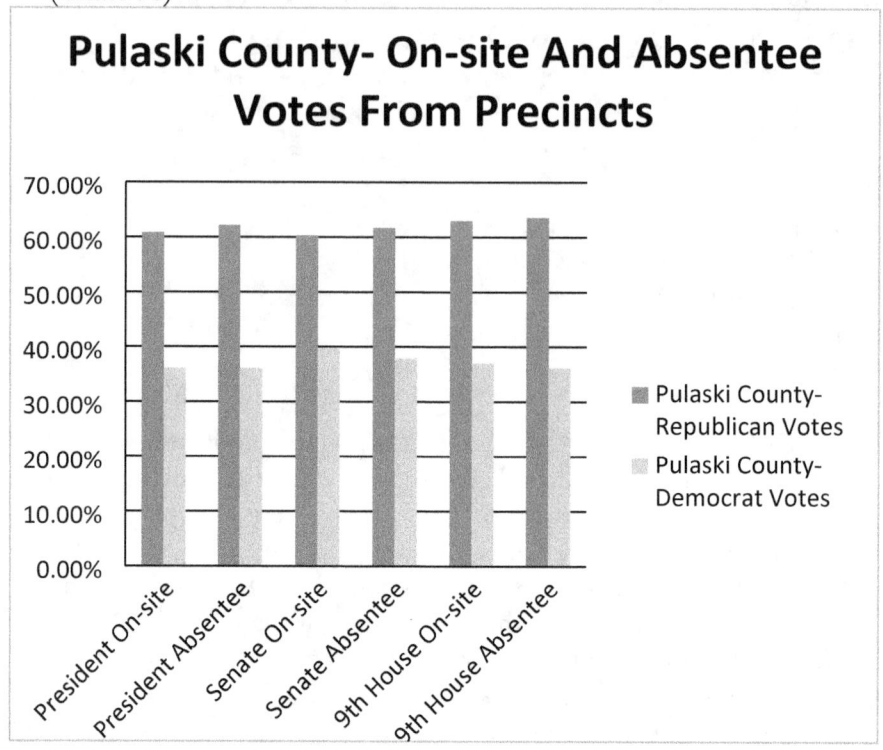

Pulaski County- On-site And Absentee Votes From Precincts

Legend:
- Pulaski County- Republican Votes
- Pulaski County- Democrat Votes

(Table 17)

Pulaski County Vote Spread Between President, Senate and House Seats On-site and Absentee

President%	Absentee%	Spread On-Site from Absentee
R) 60.76	62.10	+ 1.34
D) 36.04	36.02	- 0.02
US Senate%		
R) 60.25	61.63	+ 1.38
D) 39.61	37.88	- 1.73
9th District House%		
R) 62.95	63.51	+ 0.56
D) 36.98	36.12	- 0.86

Pulaski County is a special place for those who know it. Tucked away in the Blue Ridge between two universities, it has in the past decade carved out a niche as one of the only jurisdictions in Virginia to successfully remove a government figure by referendum for the charge of lying to the public. One can expect that if that same spirit runs their county, they will no doubt keep their performance of an honest holder of elections as their past performance shows us.

From what I can see, the only race that has any sign of interest is in the US Senate race; however, it is still within a change of mind that one could expect as the very long period of absentee voting took place. If I had a fictitious Diogenes Lamp award to hand out for honesty in elections, I would give it to the people of Pulaski County.

I would use Pulaski County as a base line for "normal" expectations when it comes to results.

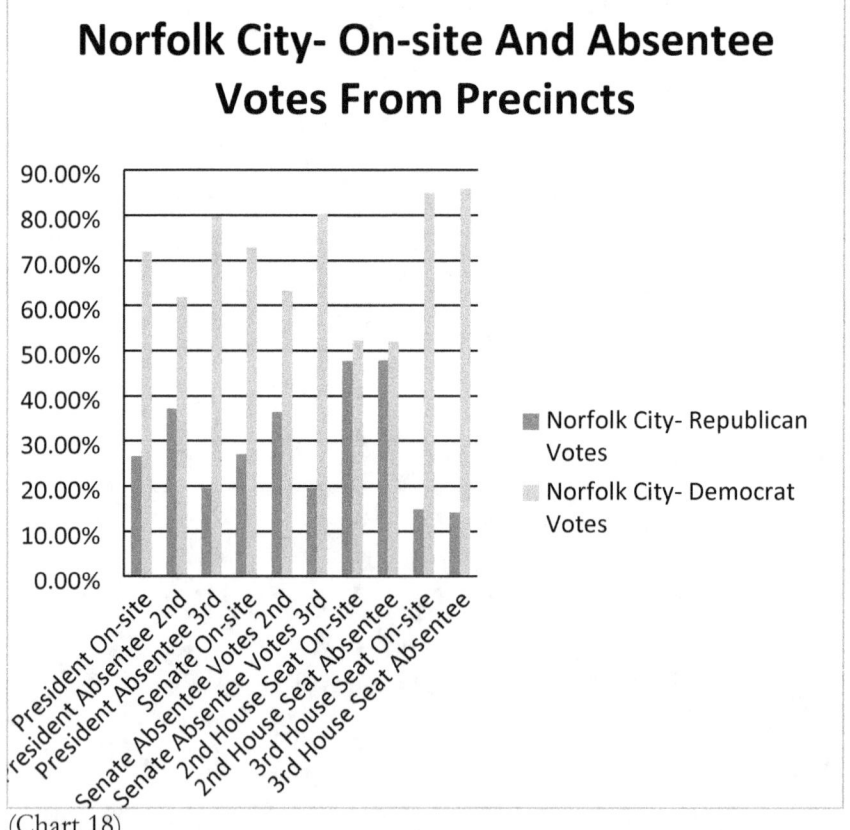

Norfolk City- On-site And Absentee Votes From Precincts

(Chart 18)

(Table 19)

Norfolk City- Vote Spread Between President, Senate and House Seats On-site and Absentee

President%	Absentee%	Spread On-Site from Absentee
R) 26.59	2nd 37.18	+10.95
D) 72.01	61.90	- 10.11
	3rd 19.55	- 7.04
	79.66	- 7.65

US Senate%		
R) 27.01	2nd 36.41	+ 9.40
D) 72.82	63.36	- 9.46
	3rd 19.52	- 7.49
	80.25	+ 7.43

2nd District House%		
R) 47.69	47.87	+ 0.18
D) 52.15	51.95	- 0.20

3rd District House%		
R) 14.85	14.11	- 0.74
D) 84.94	85.86	+ 0.92

Here we have what looks like it should not be reviewed because the results of the races are so far apart that, for the locality itself, it does not affect their interests in general. Yet, when we break down the results into the Absentee level (which was the purpose of this book) we find in the Presidential contest, the Republican candidate received 10.95% more percentage in the Absentee votes over the On-site performance in the 2nd District and 7.04% lower percentage in the Absentee tally than in the On-site results in the 3rd District.

The Democrat candidate had a 10.11% higher percentage of On-site voting over the Absentee percentage in the 2nd District. The Democrat came away with a 7.65% increase of Absentee votes over the On-site performance in the 3rd District.

In the US Senate race, the Republican had a 9.40% higher

percentage of vote's Absentee percentage than the On-site average in the 2nd District and 7.49% higher On-site performance over the Absentee performance in the 3rd District.

The Democrat had 9.46% On-site voting average over the Absentee figures in the 2nd District and 7.43% more Absentee vote average over the On-site averages.

The averages for the two House of Representative races are curiously well under the threshold limits of suspicion while the averages for the Presidential race and the US Senate in my opinion, show evidence of On-site voter fraud in the Presidential race and Absentee Voter fraud in the case of the US Senate.

(Chart 17)

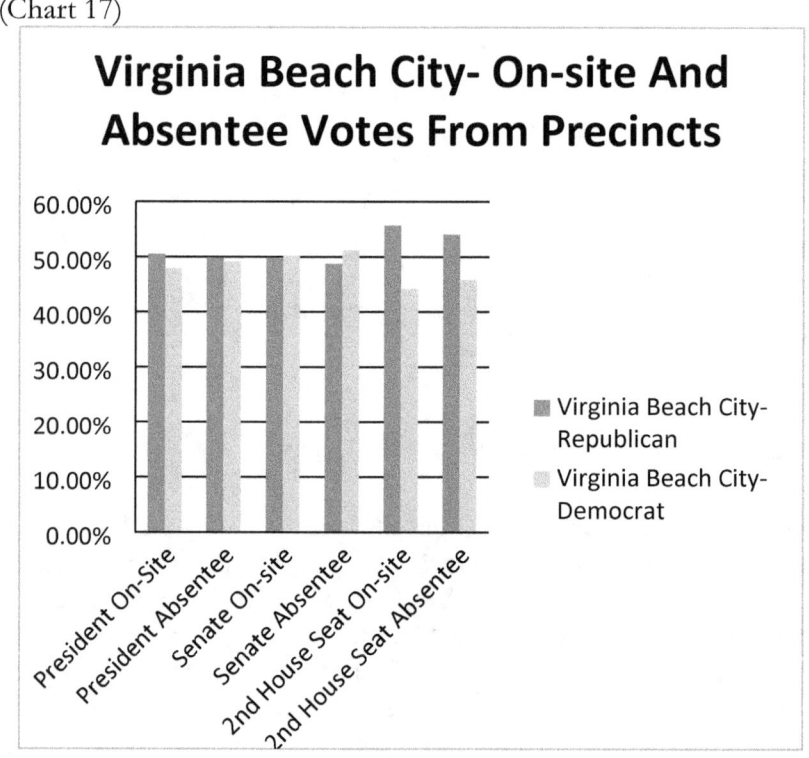

(Table 18)

Virginia Beach City- Vote Spread Between President, Senate and House Seats On-site and Absentee

President%	Absentee%	Spread On-Site from Absentee
R) 50.49	49.86	- 0.63
D) 47.95	49.14	+ 1.19
US Senate%		
R) 49.66	48.74	- 0.92
D) 50.22	51.17	+ 0.95
2nd District House%		
R) 55.70	54.04	- 1.66
D) 44.18	45.85	+ 1.67

In moving my search for differing locations across the state for results not biased against another region, I settled on the cities of Virginia Beach and Norfolk.

Using the calculation models from the previous jurisdictions, the Virginia Beach ratios between the Absentee percentages and the On-site performances fall within that threshold where you would expect a community of common interests to be. Like Pulaski County in the previous chapter, I would have to give the fictitious Diogenes Lamp Award to the City of Virginia Beach for running a clean election.

5 SUMMING UP THE POSSIBLE FRAUD

Here I will try to boil all of the statistics down to a simple list of what I believe to have identified as problems with our election process in Virginia and deliver huge, race reversing, fraudulent results from the 2012 General Election.

Sum of possible fraud per District by volume of Absentee Votes:

- ✓ 8th District: Almost twice the state average of Absentee votes
- ✓ 8th District's 3,133 mystery votes from the Voter Turnout page- where did they go? Who got them?
- ✓ 8th District's 688 more Absentee votes on the Voter Turnout page than were published in precinct levels-where did they go? Who got them?
- ✓ 10th District: Second highest and well above average
- ✓ 11th District: Almost the same as second place and well above average

Sum of possible fraud per jurisdiction:

Alexandria:
- ✓ High Volume of Absentee Voting
Arlington:
- ✓ High Volume of Absentee Voting
- ✓ High Percentage of Possible Absentee Fraud

44

Clarke County:
- ✓ High Percentage of Possible Absentee Fraud

Falls Church City:
- ✓ High Volume of Absentee Votes
- ✓ High Percentage of Possible Absentee Fraud

Fairfax City:
- ✓ Some possible Absentee Fraud

Fairfax County:
- ✓ High Volume of Absentee Votes
- ✓ High Percentage of Possible Absentee Fraud
- ✓ Unusual Volume Results in 10th District

Fauquier County:
- ✓ Probable On-Site voter fraud in the 1st District precincts (5th District no problem)

Frederick County:
- ✓ Some possible Absentee Fraud

Loudoun County: No Anomalies

Madison County:
- ✓ High Percentage of Possible Absentee Fraud

Manassas City:
- ✓ High Probability of On-site Voter Fraud

Norfolk City:
- ✓ High Probability of On-site Voter Fraud in Presidential and Senate races
- ✓ 2nd and 3rd District House races appear completely legitimate and juxtaposed to the other top races

Prince William County:
- ✓ High Probability of Possible On-site Voter Fraud
- ✓ 10th District house results unusual in the juxtaposition of the other districts

Pulaski County: No Anomalies

Virginia Beach City: No Anomalies

Winchester City:
- ✓ Unusual Volume for the winner of the 10th District House race.

By my count, there are twenty three Anomalies of possible fraud in the eighteen jurisdictions included in this study. Only three of the jurisdictions had physical voting results which mirror the percentages you would expect from a local population.

Just to make it clear, I in no way mean or wish to project any negative light on the good, average people, who live in these jurisdictions while being critical of those jurisdictions on the integrity of their election processes. My thrust here in the book is to flush out another type of person.

The types of Fraud, which you can imagine take place, are probably involving NGO's (Non-Governmental Organization) operating on donations from wealthy people or groups. They could easily bankroll an operation to build a database of dead people from insiders working in places such as senior living facilities and rehabilitation facilities. With that information, a political party could have its ranks swell year-by-year and nobody would know the difference.

Another scenario can be run by people who watch the obituaries and collect that information to generate false identifications and generate absentee votes or On-site voting identities.

Another scenario encompasses those "volunteers" who work the polls. They can work with the fraudsters with a wink and a nod. Who vouches for their integrity? The votes being counted on site are not in any way connected with computer databases, which are used to allow only registered voters into the poll. There is not one-to-one accountability.

Another scenario encompasses electronic on-site fraud which takes place by the volunteers.

Let me make this point here about my experience with volunteers, running the polls.

In one primary race I voted in, I made sure I as the first one to vote at that precinct when the doors opened, because I was also going to hand out flyers for one of the candidates in the primary.

When they unlocked the door and I was allowed in, I looked down at the manual tally sheet they had of people who voted for the Democrat and those who voted for the Republican. I saw six names on the sheet! However, I thought I was the first to vote? As I scanned the room, there were six volunteers, manning the polls. All six names were on the Democrat tally sheet. The proctor saw me looking and then I looked at him. He just had a strange smile. You cannot trust volunteers. This practice must come to an end.

Another type of fraud the good people have no control over is more on the high tech level. If our electronic votes (and the new paper vote readers transform the ballot information into electronic data) are boxed up electronically, sent to another location outside of the precinct, and has no expectation of privacy. In fact, as if Sun Tzu himself directed it, they use the strength of our private vote to cover up the electronic or mechanical fraud. They justify the secrecy of their transactions as part of our right to the secret ballot. Therefore, if we cannot see our votes, then we do not know what happens to them.

One of my favorite allegories is if you could imagine that Associations for Freeholders and Freemen and all of their counterparts of the period boxed up all of their paper ballots (the Colony of South Carolina was the inventor of the secret ballot) and sent them to the Massachusetts Bay Colony Company in England or the East India Company and had them tabulate the results, then transmit the results back to the colonies on a sheet of paper. Do you think the United States would ever have been born?

There are so many ways to commit Election Fraud or Voter Fraud and now this Electronic Mechanical Fraud, that one cannot possibly list them all. The Electronic fraud is newer and I have a feeling, that a higher hand protects specific House Seats. I think that a higher hand is located in an overseas nation where our votes are being counted and then transmitted back to us.

6 SUGGESTIONS

All I can do at this point is give you the information I was able to uncover and hope that if you do not see your location here, that you will find it and try out my models of scrutiny on those results. If you find the same results as I have, then you need to spread the word and demand action from your state legislators. You need to get them to find a judge who can either put a stop to the absentee system or confiscate all Absentee votes for complete scrutiny.

You need to get people together and volunteer to work the poles as well as watch the poles.

As for suggestions of changes, which we need I can list these:

- Get the legislature to stop absentee voting of all kinds. It is a fraud machine and we have proven it here in this book.
- Get the legislature to create a law forcing any person or institution, which is witness to anyone's death, to notify the board of elections to purge that person from the voter rolls immediately.
- When a family member passes, make sure you go to where they were registered to vote and have that registrar remove them from the voter rolls.
- Get the legislature to declare all election days are state holidays, all businesses, except for medical and emergency operations, will be closed, and there is no reason for citizens not to exercise their franchise. Those who have to work in the medical and emergency services can be allowed an absentee ballot or they can be accommodated by the BOE.

www.ingramcontent.com/pod-product-compliance
Lightning Source LLC
Chambersburg PA
CBHW060227290526
45789CB00003B/1446

- Do away with anybody handling voter registration except for the local registrar's office. Never give your personal information to somebody with a clipboard and a smile.
- Virginia National Guardsmen must man all polls including the registrar offices, and the Virginia State Police needs to be expanded as an executive section to manage the Guardsmen on the job of an election. The State Police will be directed by the State Senate.
- All electronic means of voting are to be destroyed and replaced by paper ballots of exactly the same design for the entire state.
- All precincts must close at the same time.
- All ballots must be sealed and delivered to the House of Delegates in Richmond. They must be carried under armed guard.
- The House of Delegates will have the members form a vote counting session and count all votes in an open forum.
- The members of the Electoral College will oversee the Vote counting Session. This is new for them but they must be witness to the people's suffrage.
- The results must then be presented to the Virginia Supreme Court and they will validate the results.
- The Federal Government and NGOs need to absolutely be kept out of our sovereign state and its elections.
- All Registered Voters databases need to be checked for dead people and people registered in other locations. These data bases need to be purged.

This may appear to be too large a process for just a few votes. What is at stake is much larger and we all know it.

Let us stand together and work to stop the disgrace, which we have allowed to take place over our heads and the very grounds of the man who for all intents and purposes invented the definition of the free human being. I would not be surprised if George Mason, his first and second wife, and children have probably already voted in the 2016 General Election!

Trust me: if Virginia is turning purple, it is only because a particular political party has its corrupt hands around our throats, cutting off our air. No matter what your skin color, if your oxygen is cut off, you will turn purple. It is when you die that you turn blue.

You must get involved now. It sickens me to acknowledge that our individual sovereignty and our right to a democratic collective voice for our republic have been stolen by those who do not share our community interest as defined in the Declaration of Rights. They are not going to give it back just because we ask them to.

To answer my own question on the title of this book, IT IS RIGGED!